Complete Horoscope Aquarius 2020

Monthly astrological forecasts for 2020

TATIANA BORSCH

Copyright © 2019 Tatiana Borsch.

All rights reserved. No part of this book may be reproduced, stored, or transmitted by any means—whether auditory, graphic, mechanical, or electronic—without written permission of the author, except in the case of brief excerpts used in critical articles and reviews. Unauthorized reproduction of any part of this work is illegal and is punishable by law.

Because of the dynamic nature of the Internet, any web addresses or links contained in this book may have changed since publication and may no longer be valid. The views expressed in this work are solely those of the author and do not necessarily reflect the views of the publisher, and the publisher hereby disclaims any responsibility for them.

This book is a work of non-fiction. Unless otherwise noted, the author and the publisher make no explicit guarantees as to the accuracy of the information contained in this book and in some cases, names of people and places have been altered to protect their privacy.

Any people depicted in stock imagery provided by Getty Images are models, and such images are being used for illustrative purposes only.
Certain stock imagery © Getty Images.

CONTENTS

GENERAL FORECAST FOR AQUARIUS VII
JANUARY 1
FEBRUARY 3
MARCH 5
APRIL 7
MAY 9
JUNE 11
JULY 13
AUGUST 15
SEPTEMBER 17
OCTOBER 19
NOVEMBER 21
DECEMBER 23
ZODIAC CONNECTIONS AND US - A GUIDE TO COMPATIBILITY (COMPATIBILITY OF ZODIAC SIGNS) 25

General Forecast for Aquarius

2020 will be a difficult year with a lot of changes. The key thing is to change your old and tired ways and to plan for your future.

Business. In the first half of the year, many Aquarians will be busy with the preparation of new projects. Entrepreneurs and managers of all levels will do a good piece of property business and their business will expand. There will be, however, numerous issues connected to face in this period.

For clerical workers, the first half of the year is quite tranquil, although many of you start planning a job change; you will make it fly but only next year, in 2021.

The second part of the year is less tranquil. During this period, you will reconsider your plans and the situation will then start to look more realistic. Those whose interests are connected to partners from other cities and overseas will face serious problems. Overseas colleagues will behave in an aggressive manner and this will unsurprisingly cause tensions. The root of the problem might be property or land and the resulting, acute struggle will last from June to December 2020.

In other cases, there will be possible legal problems, inspections and checks; these will be difficult to resolve. However, by the end of 2021 you will reach a good compromise allowing you to escape any troubling circumstances.

Money. Financially, the first half of the year is stable. You may have income from different sources, and it will likely increase. Builders and those whose business is real estate or land will be especially successful.

Those not involved in business can rely on the support of parents, close friends and relatives. You might come into an inheritance or sell your property at a good price.

The second half of the year is less favourable and shows a decline in income and a growth in expenses. In some cases, it is connected to problems in business. In other cases, with troubles in your personal life.

Love and family. Many families might completely change their way of life. You may make a major renovation to your house or you may buy or sell a flat, a house or a country house. If you have such plans you should involve lawyers in order to comply with the letter of the law; otherwise you will have to deal with extended problems.

Those who own property abroad should also be cautious. In the second part of the year, international tensions might put your ownership of the property into question.

You might be involved in a spate of conflicts with your relatives. There might also be a long conflict with a particular relative, or a difficult situation with a close friend.

For romantic affairs this year is neutral with nothing extraordinary forecast to happen.

However, if the person you love lives abroad, you will face problems in the second half of the year that will not finish before December.

Health. Your energy levels are not high in 2020 and for this reason you should take care of yourself and keep to your limits. It is possible that you will have to take care of some family members; try to consider all possible options and take any necessary steps in advance. In the second part of the year, you should also be more careful while driving, as the chances of accidents and injuries are quite high.

COMPLETE HOROSCOPE 2020

JANUARY

January is downtime. The stars recommend that you start saving your energy and limiting yourself to safe, routine activity.

Business. The Christmas holiday must have had a relaxing effect on you. This is not a bad period for you, but starting any serious deals is not recommended - the best you can hope for is to get your ducks in a row and to weigh up your future actions.

Entrepreneurs and managers will start changing their business and this might be the expansion of a business or laying the groundwork for further business development.

You might enter into various property deals; either an advantageous purchase or a profitable sale.

You might move your business to a different city or just to new premises. Your relations with partners are harmonious, but closer to the end of the month financial disagreements become possible.

Clerical workers may have to face changes in their company - such as a change in management or redeployment - that push you to change your job and to look elsewhere to use your skills. You will definitely find such a place, if not this month then later.

Money. The financial situation is stable, and you will have regular income; not necessarily from your main job. You might make a profit from real estate. You are likely to get good terms on a loan or savings.

If you are not involved in business, you might get help from your parents or partner. You might come into an inheritance. At the end of the month, you might expect heavy expenses connected to your personal life or to your friends and business partners.

Family and love. In most cases, all the key events will take place within your family and your home. You might expect serious changes connected to property - either buying, selling or renovating your home. Some of your birth sign will do this in January, others in other months of 2020.

Family relations are quite balanced. Strong couples, being wise and loving, will overcome various domestic problems together.

Couples in a romantic relationship might face some difficulties in the last ten days of January. They might have misunderstandings and arguments due to differing views on life and, which is maybe worse, financial problems. However, it should be said that all these problems can be sorted out if there is the mutual desire to do so.

Health. Your energy levels are not high in January. There are unfavourable days on the full moon days of the 9th to the 11th, and also the 22nd to the 25th. During these periods you should take more care of yourself and keep strictly to your limits. You should be careful when driving and avoid dangerous situations.

FEBRUARY

Events will allow you to see your life from a different angle. Good luck!

Business. The first half of February is busy and dynamic. Entrepreneurs and managers will continue the revitalization of their business and possibly start looking for new space into which to expand.

Co-operation with partners from other cities and overseas is developing well and you might have a trip, lucrative negotiations or agreements to co-operate. Those involved in construction or the real estate business will have very good income, and all organizational problems will be successfully resolved.

Clerical workers will take an active part in corporate restructuring and your efforts will be noticed and duly appreciated.

The second part of the month does not look so good. Many problems, mainly financial issues, will be discussed at length but there is nothing extraordinary in this. Between the 17th of February and the 10th of March, you will have to weigh up all the possible variants and probably make changes to your current plans. After this, everything will slip into a better groove.

Money. The financial situation remains stable. Many of your birth sign will profit from real estate activities and some of you may come into an inheritance.

You might also expect financial support from your parents or family members.

Love and family. You are coming into a period of renewal in your personal life. For some it will affect your daily household routine, for others it will affect family matters.

In the first case, there is likely to be major refurbishment or renovation of your flat and perhaps even the purchase or sale of accommodation. In the second case, you will re-evaluate your family relationships.

In both cases you should not worry about the changes to come because they will drive you forward. This is also true for those who plan to move to a new city or abroad.

The stars advise you to be more cautious in executing real estate transactions, signing paperwork or transferring money in the period from the 17th of February to the 10th of March. The best tactics will be to analyse the situation and then to sign documents and transfer money only after the 10th of March. In this way you will avoid errors, deceit and losses.

Health. February is your month. Your energy levels will be high and all problems with health stay away from you.

MARCH

All those problems you have been trying to solve for some time will be easily resolved this month. It looks like you have reached the necessary level of understanding.

Business. The first ten days of March are important and practical. Entrepreneurs and managers of various levels will be busy solving financial matters and the stars recommend you be more cautious as the possibility of making mistakes is quite high during the first ten days of March. It is wiser to spend this time discussing and analysing the current situation and to then make decisions in the second half of the month. In this way, you will achieve maximum success and profit.

The second half of the month is a very positive and productive period when all your most ambitious plans and wildest dreams might well come true. If you plan to expand your business, you can expect good results and use this period to your advantage.

Those whose business is connected to property, land and construction will be especially successful.

Clerical workers will be able to improve their professional and financial situations and the ideal time for this is in the second half of March.

Money. The financial situation is stable with a good chance of an upswing. You will have regular cash inflows and not only from your official place of employment. Many of your birth sign will receive income from selling or leasing out property. Those who plan to sell a business can also expect to profit.

Love and family. Those who live with a partner will spend most of March doing domestic work and solving organisational problems. It is possible that you will move to a new house, finish the renovation of your current home or buy new furniture to refurbish your home. It is also possible that you will sell your house or flat at a profit.

Married couples might be going through changes in their relationship. Even such difficult situations as splitting up and division of property might be resolved without conflict or bitterness.

Couples who have had a long romantic relationship might decide to live together and parents or senior members of the family could assist in this matter.

Many families can expect an addition to their family, and this might happen in March.

Health. Your energy levels are not high this month, but if you live a healthy lifestyle you will not have any serious problems with your health. Many Aquarians tend to gain weight easily and so it is worth keeping to a diet, going to the gym more often and remembering that walks in the countryside are also very useful.

You should be extra careful to details - fastidious and meticulous. Only this way will you be able to achieve your goals and avoid silly mistakes this month.

Business. The first twenty days of April will be a worrying and not very pleasant period. Entrepreneurs and managers should prepare for various inspections that come like a bolt out of the blue and cause any number of problems.

In a different scenario, you might face unexpected problems with colleagues from other cities or overseas; some of which might be of a legislative nature. Many of your birth sign might have to sort out difficult property situations, or correct documents and past mistakes. You should be prepared for some problems that you have ignored in the past to suddenly crop up and bite you this month. It is also possible that some information, which you would prefer to keep secret, will leak. You should take this information into account, check the weaker points of your work and take any necessary measures. As they say, 'forewarned is forearmed'.

The last week of April is quiet and stable. All of the problems from the first half of the month are now being sorted out one way or another. This positive process will continue into May.

Money. This month is more or less neutral financially. You should not expect big expenses, but neither will you earn a great deal. Only during the last week of the month can you expect income from successful property deals or from a loan on very favourable terms.

Love and family. Many Aquarians will have very important events in their personal life. Many families might be faced with a difficult situation regarding property and it is possible that you will have conflicts with relatives. If you plan to sell, buy, or rent your property, April is not the best time for this. You should postpone your decision until the last week of April or the first half of May - this should allow you to eliminate any mistakes and misunderstandings.

Your children not only make you happy, they might become a real source of support in all of this month's troubles.

Relations between lovers are harmonious; your partner is calm, tactful and ready to help you.

Health. Your energy levels are quite high this month. The stars recommend you be more cautious whilst travelling and driving as the chances of accidents and unpleasant events are quite high in the first twenty days of April.

Most of May will be quiet, creative and even romantic. There is nothing wrong with that - sometimes it is useful to forget about work.

Business. May is not so quiet for those whose business involves land, real estate and construction. They have lucrative contracts and will make a good profit.

Others might spend the first half of May having a rest and being busy with family and household activities.

The second half of the month is not really favourable for business. During this period you are not immune from mistakes and misfortunes. You should not put your skin in the game and make any hasty decisions - this is especially true in financial matters as risks here might incur serious losses.

Money. The first half of the month is quite stable. You might make additional profit from real estate or your business partners. Close friends or relatives might also give you financial support. There is the possibility of coming into an inheritance.

The situation will change drastically in the second half of May. During this period your expenses will grow - in some cases it will be due to business needs, in other cases, it will be related to family needs. People who are involved with finances should be extra prudent as the possibility of losses is high this month.

Love and family. The best place to devote your energy this month is starting to refurnish and renovate your accommodation.

During this period, family relations are harmonious. Strong couples will find solutions to various domestic and household situations. Those who plan to sell or to buy house can do this profitably during the period from the 1st to the 13th of May.

The second half of May will not be very successful. Resentment between lovers over finances, morals and life choices may become conflict and may continue into June.

During the second half of the month parents might have problems with children. A substantial part of the family budget will be spent on solving these problems.

Health. This month your energy levels are quite high and there is no need to worry about your health.

Do not be over-critical of those around you as it will not help you to avoid conflicts, misunderstandings and other problems. This advice is true for both work and for love.

Business. It will be quite difficult to focus on all the matters at hand this month. The usual errands might be challenging, all-consuming and still not get finished. You should pay extra attention to financial matters because there are some problems in this area - you might be faced with unexpected costs as a result of general instability or even chaos in your business.

Managers should be attentive to their employees in the second half of the month as they might not behave responsibly or carry out their work competently. During this period clerical workers will face tensions and underhand deals among fellow members of staff. It will be difficult to sort out all the situations, so do not jump to ill-judged conclusions and try to avoid conflict. You should also remember that not everything said is true, and that many decisions taken in June will have to be reconsidered later. All professionally active Aquarians, irrespective of their line of work, should take this into account.

Money. The financial situation is not stable. You will haemorrhage money regularly due either to work or to your personal life.

The astrologer advises you to be extra cautious because Mars, known as an aggressive planet, is in the financial sector at the moment.

Those who are directly involved in finance – accountants, bankers, brokers and so on – should be more than cautious. You cannot expect a profit this month, and financial losses are quite possible.

Love and family. You might face some difficulties in your personal life too. Parents will have to sort out their children's problems and invest a substantial part of the family budget in their education, a holiday or other miscellaneous expenses. The stars recommend that you consider all such expenditure thoroughly because you might well over-spend.

You should also be careful with your other expenses; June is not the best of times for expensive purchases and major investments.

Many loving couples might start or continue to grow apart or perhaps even fall out unexpectedly. This is a difficult time in all respects, so keep your head and do not go shooting from the hip. It is very difficult to determine just who is right and who is wrong at the moment. If something is not right in your relationship, try to explain your concerns tactfully or perhaps just take a break.

Health. You are in good health this month and positively brimming with energy if a bit over-anxious and fidgety. If you do get tired, there should be no problem in having a couple of days break in order to escape the routine and the humdrum.

COMPLETE HOROSCOPE 2020

July is quite difficult. The main trend is a large amount of work that brings neither joy nor pleasure.

Business. As the first half of the month is an unclear and quite tense time, you should not plan anything important for this period. It is likely that you will still be fighting off various problems from last month.

Entrepreneurs and managers might become the object of an over-zealous interest from the authorities. The stars highly recommend that you prepare for inspections as you are unlikely to be happy with the results otherwise. It is possible that some information emerges which really should have been kept secret.

Those whose business is connected with colleagues from other cities and overseas might experience some complications. Various misunderstandings, emergencies or legal problems are possible.

Clerical workers might find it very difficult to work in an environment where there is conflict or even poisonous assignation within the body of staff. In the worst-case scenario, it might even come to their dismissal.

Managers of all levels should keep their employees on a tight leash because their work is far from perfect.

Money. Financially, the situation looks neutral. Money will come in as it did last month and nothing unexpected will happen, at least for the time being.

Love and family. Those whose focus is their personal life will suffer some difficult times. There might be some serious problems with your relatives – an argument or other issues with your closest relatives. Some of your close relatives might fall ill and you will have to take an active part in their treatment.

Looking further ahead, we may say that most of your current problems will be sorted out in August and the rest in September.

Lovers might unexpectedly fall out or not see each other as often as they would like.

All Aquarians should be alert that some unpleasant secrets might emerge in July.

Health. Those who luckily escape professional and personal troubles might have problems with their health. Take care and visit a good physician if necessary but under no circumstances should you self-medicate.

You should also be careful while driving and during trips. Avoid dangerous situations as the possibility of accident and injury is quite high this month.

AUGUST

Do not try to solve all your problems by yourself. The Arab saying, 'one hand cannot clap' is an appropriate one for August.

Business. August is a good time to somehow solve the problems of recent months which either relate to inspections or legal problems or to situations with colleagues from other cities and overseas.

In any case, you will be able to alleviate the situation but only by addressing your allies or other competent consultants.

You should use all the opportunities presented to you and tackle the problems step by step; cautiously and prudently. Although you cannot expect complete success, you will be able to achieve much, and this is better than nothing.

Real estate deals continue and you might expect a genuine breakthrough at the end of August or in the first ten days of September. During this period, you might receive some new proposals and many of the issues that have been bothering you will quickly be resolved.

Money. The financial situation is not quite stable for the first twenty days of August whereas the last week of the month and the first week of September will be more successful. During this period, you might profit from beneficial real estate transactions or the receipt of a loan. Those not involved in business might expect the support of parents or loved ones.

Love and family. The situation in your personal life will also improve.

Complications between close relatives become more understandable and easier to solve as a result. It is possible that your spouse or partner will help you with the more difficult issues and also with situations when your relatives are faced with troubles or serious mischief.

Happily married couples might be busy solving problems connected with either purchasing or selling real estate.

Health. Your energy levels are not high this month, so you need to take care of yourself, hustle less and remember the benefits of a good's sleep.

You should be cautious when traveling and driving as there is still the risk of accident and injury.

SEPTEMBER

September is a routine, working month. Take a breather! Opportunities just around the corner might rock your world and you need to be energized and prepared for them.

Business. It is better to rest and busy yourself with personal matters in September. However, if you are a workaholic, and your work always comes first, you can put your matters in order; carry out some organizational duties and fix any outstanding problems related to old legal issues and tensions with authorities and their inspections.

In a different scenario, the problems might lie in a long-standing conflict with colleagues from other cities or overseas or with paperwork and red tape. At present, all the issues are fundamental to your business and it is unlikely that you will be able to resolve them quickly.

Nevertheless, you will have to deal with the situation because you have no choice; it is quite serious and might require your attention once again in the near future.

Money. The financial situation is stable. You might have additional income from various real estate deals and from various lines of credit or easy-term loans.

You are very likely to come into an inheritance. Those involved in construction or the real estate and land industry will be especially successful.

Love and family. Many Aquarians will see the main events of September happen at home and in their family. There might be changes to the household, some of them only slight; perhaps finishing a permanent repair, a house-warming party or perhaps selling or exchanging a property.

Problems with your relatives continue. The astrologer sees these problems as being so serious that they cannot be resolved overnight; you will need to spend a few months working at these issues.

Lovers might suffer from the effects of rumor and gossip and the stars highly recommend safeguarding your relationship against any intrusion by strangers.

Health. Your energy levels are not high this month, so take care of yourself and keep to your limits. You should also be aware of the possibility of putting on weight, so remember the benefits of a balanced diet. You should also be more careful on trips and while driving as the possibility of accidents and unpleasant situations on the road is still there in September.

COMPLETE HOROSCOPE 2020

OCTOBER

You really want to move forward this month, but the circumstances actually warrant stopping. Even if you do have to take a step back, remember that your goals are achievable!

Business. Many Aquarians will again face problems arising from the past in October. These may be either complicated relationships with your colleagues from other cities or overseas or legal problems. The situation looks more demanding this time and it seems that you are at a stalemate. The problems will, in fact, linger on but one cannot say that they are unmanageable. The sky will clear in a couple of months, so don't give up but keep addressing your current issues one by one. You should always bear in mind the old words of wisdom, still true today, 'A journey of a thousand miles begins with a single step'.

The stars also recommend being attentive to those around you. It is possible that your enemies, both overt and covert, will become especially active. They will be up to no good and try to discover some of your secrets; you should stand fast and not give such venomous people any reason to gossip and spread conspiracies.

Clerical workers will be faced with changes at work, but the astrologer has good reason to believe that they will lead to benefits rather than drawbacks.

Money. The financial situation is stable this month and it seems that your professional problems do not affect your finances – this is a good thing. Your income and expenses in October are sensible and predictable.

Love and family. In your personal life, events originating in the past will further develop. The main issue is that problems with relatives are not only remain unsolved but appear to be heating up. The circumstances might appear different; there might be a serious, long-term argument or troubles that have been visited upon one of your family members.

The situation for lovers will be no better. Some malicious actors might interfere in their relationship and reveal things they wished to remain secret.

Married couples will continue to improve their home and this process seems to be reaching its end.

Health. Your energy levels are not high this month. Those suffering from migraines or chronic heart disease or those generally under the weather will be at risk.

Drivers and those traveling should be extra cautious this month as the danger of accidents is very high. It is better to cancel all trips this month as they might not go the way you had planned and dreamed.

NOVEMBER

You have been working hard recently and you can now see your goal ahead of you. This month and those ahead are good for taking action. So, don't sit back and do nothing but square up to any difficulties.

Business. You will be at your peak in November and able to move mountains, or at least to solve the problems of recent months much more easily. This is true for both those who have been dealing with the authorities and their inspections and those who have been trying to sort out various legal questions.

Relationships with colleagues from other cities or overseas are developing with varying degrees of success. You still have problems, but towards the end of November it will become clear that they are all quite manageable. Indeed, most of the complicated issues which have been worrying you recently will be sorted out one way or another in December.

Money. The financial situation looks good this month with regular inflows of money in increased amounts. The approximate dates for the receipt of large sums of money are the 5th, 6th, 14th, 15th, and the 22nd to the 24th of November.

Love and family. Your personal life is less important to you than work this month. Nevertheless, those whose life is centered on love and family will face the same old problems again this month. Your relationships with your relatives remain tricky and there might well be fiery outbursts due to pernicious disagreements or to the frustratingly endless troubles of someone close to you.

Those moving faraway will continue to deal with various problems and will succeed with many of them in November.

Lovers might feel uncomfortable in November. The past few months have revealed many things to you and the problems you once managed to sidestep now demand your serious attention. You might have to make a decision that is unlikely to be a positive one; if your fortune should point you in a different direction, it will only be for the better.

Health. You are healthy, active and ready to move mountains in November and without a shadow of doubt, these qualities are very necessary at the moment.

DECEMBER

You fall under the influence of two powerful planets - Jupiter and Saturn - in December. They open your eyes to both the past and to the future. Such co-incidences in the zodiac are very rare and if your fortune should indicate a path to you, follow it without reservation.

Business. A complicated period in your life is finished: this is equally true for those who have faced aggression from their partners from other cities or overseas; for those who have had a conflict with the authorities and their inspections or for those who have had prolonged legal issues. The battles are finally coming to their logical conclusion and you will now have a chance to get on with your business or to start something new; you need to be in good shape and totally prepared, however.

Opportunities that only begin to show themselves in the second part of December will fully unfurl next year. It is natural that these opportunities demand serious effort and responsibility of you. As your future depends on your decisions, you need to think everything through properly.

Money. December will be rather neutral financially; you cannot expect big earnings, but your expenses will be moderate and sensible.

Love and family. For those whose life is centered around love or family, the stars promise peace and tranquillity.

Your relationships with relatives who experienced grave situations in their lives eventually stabilize; there are reasons to believe that you will reconcile and that the protracted problems among your close relatives will cease. The situation is improving, but you will face other problems - this time connected to real estate - in the near future.

This will happen in 2021 and so you need to consider all the possible variants and take measures so as not to be caught flat footed.

Health. Even though your energy levels are quite high this month, you should be extra careful while driving and traveling between the 20th and the 25th of December.

Zodiac connections and us - a guide to compatibility

Often, when we meet a person, we get a feeling that they are good and we take an instant liking to them. Another person, however, gives us immediate feelings of distrust, fear and hostility. Is there an astrological reason why people say that 'the first impression is the most accurate'? How can we detect those who will bring us nothing but trouble and unhappiness?

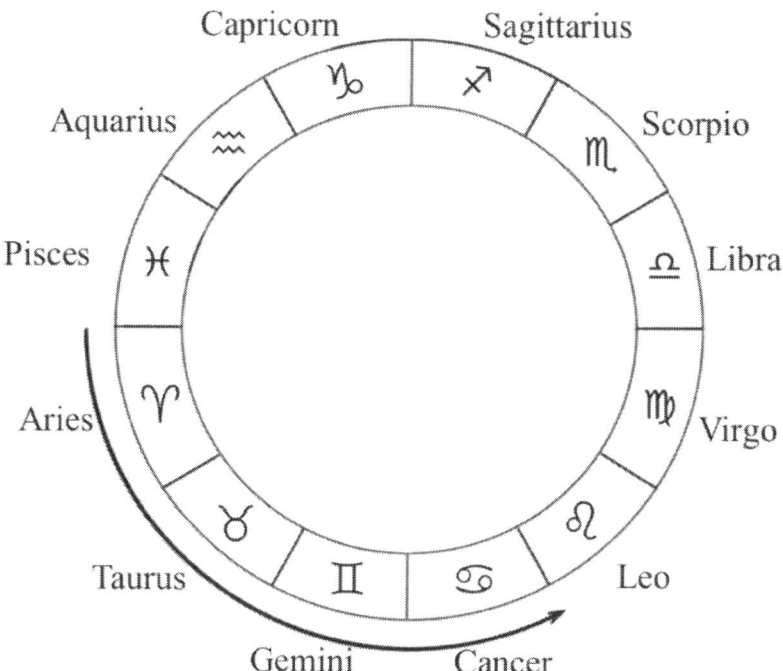

Without going too deeply into astrological subtleties unfamiliar to some readers, it is possible to determine the traits according to which friendship, love or business relationships will develop.

Let's begin with problematic relationships - our most difficult are with our 8th sign. For example, for Aries the 8th sign is Scorpio, for Taurus it is Sagittarius and so on. Finding your 8th sign is easy; assume your own sign to be first (see above Figure) and then move eight signs counter clockwise around the Zodiac circle. This is also how the other signs (fourth, ninth and so on) that we mention are to be found.

Ancient astrologers variously referred to the 8th sign as the symbol of death, of destruction, of fated love or unfathomable attraction. In astrological terms, this pair is called 'master and slave' or 'boa constrictor and rabbit', with the role of 'master' or 'boa constrictor' being played by our 8th sign.

This relationship is especially difficult for politicians and business people. We can take the example of a recent political confrontation in the USA. Hilary Clinton is a Scorpio while Donald Trump is a Gemini - her 8th sign. Even though many were certain that Clinton would be elected President, she lost.

To take another example, Hitler was a Taurus and his opponents – Stalin and Churchill - were both of his 8th sign, Sagittarius. The result of their confrontation is well known. Interestingly, the Russian Marshals who dealt crushing military blows to Hitler and so helped end the Third Reich - Konstantin Rokossovsky and Georgy Zhukov - were also Sagittarian, Hitler's 8th sign.

In another historical illustration, Lenin was also a Taurus. Stalin was of Lenin's 8th sign and was ultimately responsible for the downfall and possibly death of his one-time comrade-in-arms.

Business ties with those of our 8th sign are hazardous as they ultimately lead to stress and loss; both financial and moral. So, do not tangle with your 8th sign and never fight with it - your chances of winning are remote! Such relationships are very interesting in terms of love and romance, however. We are magnetically attracted to our 8th sign and even though it may be very intense physically, it is very difficult for family life; 'Feeling bad when together, feeling worse when apart'.

As an example, let us take the famous lovers - George Sand who was Cancer and Alfred de Musset who was Sagittarius. Cancer is the 8th sign for

Sagittarius, and the story of their crazy two-year love affair was the subject of much attention throughout France. Critics and writers were divided into 'Mussulist' and 'Sandist' camps; they debated fiercely about who was to blame for the sad ending to their love story - him or her. It's hard to imagine the energy needed to captivate the public for so long, but that energy was destructive for the couple. Passion raged in their hearts, but neither of them was able to comprehend their situation.

Georges Sand wrote to Musset, "I don't love you anymore, and I will always adore you. I don't want you anymore, and I can't do without you. It seems that nothing but a heavenly lightning strike can heal me by destroying me. Good-bye! Stay or go, but don't say that I am not suffering. This is the only thing that can make me suffer even more, my love, my life, my blood! Go away, but kill me, leaving." Musset replied only in brief, but its power surpassed Sand's tirade, "When you embraced me, I felt something that is still bothering me, making it impossible for me to approach another woman." These two people loved each other passionately and for two years lived together in a powder keg of passion, hatred and treachery.

When someone enters into a romantic liaison with their 8th sign, there will be no peace; indeed, these relationships are very attractive to those who enjoy the edgy, the borderline and, in the Dostoevsky style, the melodramatic. The first to lose interest in the relationship is, as a rule, the 8th sign.

If, by turn of fate, our child is born under our 8th sign, they will be very different from us and, in some ways, not live up to our expectations. It may be best to let them choose their own path.

In business and political relationships, the combination with our 12th sign is also a complicated one.

We can take two political examples. Angela Merkel is a Cancer while Donald Trump is a Gemini - her 12th sign. This is why their relations are strained and complicated and we can even perhaps assume that the American president will achieve his political goals at her expense. Boris Yeltsin (Aquarius) was the 12th sign to Mikhail Gorbachev (Pisces) and it was Yeltsin who managed to dethrone the champion of Perestroika.

Even ancient astrologers noticed that our relationships with our 12th signs can never develop evenly; it is one of the most curious and problematic combinations. They are our hidden enemies and they seem to be digging a hole for us; they ingratiate themselves with us, discover our innermost secrets. As a result, we become bewildered and make mistakes when we deal with them. Among the Roman emperors murdered by members of their entourage, there was an interesting pattern - all the murderers were the 12th sign of the murdered.

We can also see this pernicious effect in Russian history: the German princess Alexandra (Gemini) married the last Russian Tsar Nicholas II (Taurus) - he was her 12th sign and brought her a tragic death. The wicked genius Grigory Rasputin (Cancer) made friends with Tsarina Alexandra, who was his 12th sign, and was murdered as a result of their odd friendship. The weakness of Nicholas II was exposed, and his authority reduced after the death of the economic and social reformer Pyotr Stolypin, who was his 12th sign. Thus, we see a chain of people whose downfall was brought about by their 12th sign.

So, it makes sense to be cautious of your 12th sign, especially if you have business ties. Usually, these people know much more about us than we want them to and they will often reveal our secrets for personal gain if it suits them. However, the outset of these relationships is, as a rule, quite normal - sometimes the two people will be friends, but sooner or later one will betray the other one or divulge a secret; inadvertently or not.

In terms of romantic relationships, our 12th sign is gentle, they take care of us and are tender towards us. They know our weaknesses well but accept them with understanding. It is they who guide us, although sometimes almost imperceptibly. Sexual attraction is usually strong.
For example, Meghan Markle is a Leo, the 12th sign for Prince Harry, who is a Virgo. Despite Queen Elizabeth II being lukewarm about the match, Harry's love was so strong that they did marry.

If a child is our 12th sign, it later becomes clear that they know all our secrets, even those that they are not supposed to know. It is very difficult to control them as they do everything in their own way.
Relations with our 7th sign are also interesting. They are like our opposite; they have something to learn from us while we, in turn, have something to learn from them. This combination, in business and personal relationships, can be very positive and stimulating provided that both partners

are quite intelligent and have high moral standards but if not, constant misunderstandings and challenges follow. Marriage or co-operation with the 7th sign can only exist as the union of two fully-fledged individuals and in this case love, significant business achievements and social success are possible.

However, the combination can be not only interesting, but also quite complicated.

An example is Angelina Jolie, a Gemini, and Brad Pitt, a Sagittarius. This is a typical bond with a 7th sign - it's lively and interesting, but rather stressful. Although such a couple may quarrel and even part from time to time, never do they lose interest in each other.

This may be why this combination is more stable in middle-age when there is an understanding of the true nature of marriage and partnership. In global, political terms, this suggests a state of eternal tension - a cold war - for example between Yeltsin (Aquarius) and Bill Clinton (Leo).

Relations with our 9th sign are very good; they are our teacher and advisor - one who reveals things we are unaware of and our relationships with them very often involve travel or re-location. The combination can lead to spiritual growth and can be beneficial in terms of business.

Although, for example, Trump and Putin are political opponents, they can come to an understanding and even feel a certain sympathy for each other because Putin is a Libra while Trump is a Gemini, his 9th sign.

This union is also quite harmonious for conjugal and romantic relationships.

We treat our 3rd sign somewhat condescendingly. They are like our younger siblings; we teach them and expect them to listen attentively. Our younger brothers and sisters are more often than not born under this sign. In terms of personal and sexual relationships, the union is not very inspiring and can end quickly, although this is not always the case. In terms of business, it is fairly average as it often connects partners from different cities or countries.

We treat our 5th sign as a child and we must take care of them accordingly. The combination is not very good for business, however, since our 5th sign triumphs over us in terms of connections and finances, and thereby gives us very little in return save for love or sympathy. However, they are very good for family and romantic relationships, especially if the 5th sign is female. If a child is born as a 5th sign to their parents, their relationship will be a mutually smooth, loving and understanding one that lasts a lifetime.

Our 10th sign is a born leader. Depending on the spiritual level of those involved, both pleasant and tense relations are possible; the relationship is often mutually beneficial in the good times but mutually disruptive in the bad times. In family relations, our 10th sign always tries to lead and will do so according to their intelligence and upbringing.

Our 4th sign protects our home and can act as a sponsor to strengthen our financial or moral positions. Their advice should be heeded in all cases as it can be very effective, albeit very unobtrusive. If a woman takes this role, the relationship can be long and romantic, since all the spouse's wishes are usually met one way or another. Sometimes, such couples achieve great social success; for instance, Hilary Clinton, a Scorpio is the 4th sign to Bill Clinton, a Leo. On the other hand, if the husband is the 4th sign for his wife, he tends to be henpecked. There is often a strong sexual attraction. Our 4th sign can improve our living conditions and care for us in a parental way. If a child is our 4th sign, they are close to us and support us affectionately.

Relations with our 11th sign are often either friendly or patronizing; we treat them reverently, while they treat us with friendly condescension. Sometimes, these relationships develop in an 'older brother' or 'high-ranking friend' sense; indeed, older brothers and sisters are often our 11th sign. In terms of personal and sexual relationships, our 11th sign is always inclined to enslave us. This tendency is most clearly manifested in such alliances as Capricorn and Pisces or Leo and Libra. A child who is the 11th sign to their parents will achieve greater success than their parents, but this will only make the parents proud.

Our 2nd sign should bring us financial or other benefits; we receive a lot from them in both our business and our family life. In married couples, the 2nd sign usually looks after the financial situation for the benefit of the family. Sexual attraction is strong.

Our 6th sign is our 'slave'; we always benefit from working with them and it's very difficult for them to escape our influence. In the event of hostility, especially if they have provoked the conflict, they receive a powerful retaliatory strike. In personal relations, we can almost destroy them by making them dance to our tune. For example, if a husband doesn't allow his wife to work or there are other adverse family circumstances, she gradually becomes lost as an individual despite being surrounded by care. This is the best-case scenario; worse outcomes are possible. Our 6th sign has a strong sexual attraction to us because we are the fatal 8th sign for them; we cool down quickly, however, and often make all kinds of demands. If the relationship with our 6th sign is a long one, there is a danger that routine, boredom and stagnation will ultimately destroy the relationship. A child born under our 6th sign needs particularly careful handling as they can feel fear or embarrassment when communicating with us. Their health often needs increased attention and we should also remember that they are very different from us emotionally.

Finally, we turn to relations with our own sign. Scorpio with Scorpio and Cancer with Cancer get along well, but in most other cases, however, our own sign is of little interest to us as it has a similar energy. Sometimes, this relationship can develop as a rivalry, either in business or in love.

There is another interesting detail - we are often attracted to one particular sign. For example, a man's wife and mistress often have the same sign. If there is confrontation between the two, the stronger character displaces the weaker one. As an example, Prince Charles is a Scorpio, while both Princess Diana and Camilla Parker Bowles were born under the sign of Cancer. Camilla was the more assertive and became dominant.

Of course, in order to draw any definitive conclusions, we need an individually prepared horoscope, but the above always, one way or another, manifests itself.

Tatiana Borsch

Made in the USA
San Bernardino, CA
24 November 2019